Catch Phat Air! Ride Fakie! Epic!

Those awesome rhinos who tore up the waves in *Rhinos Who Surf* are hitting the slopes—and snowboarding has never been so much fun! Readers will delight in following these adorable rhinos as they grab their boards in search of fresh snow. With totally cool pictures and radically useful snowboard lingo, *Rhinos Who Snowboard* is killer reading for boarders and snow-lovers of every age.

"Bright, stylized drawings . . . capture the action." *–School Library Journal*

To my sisters, who are also my best friends,
Jill Swistak, Gina Schneider, and Linda Mammano

With special thanks to California Board Shop
and James Adkins

First paperback edition published in 2004
by Chronicle Books LLC.

Book design by Lucy Nielsen.
Typeset in Gills Sans.
Manufactured in Hong Kong.
ISBN 0-8118-4570-2

The Library of Congress has catalogued the hardcover edition
as follows:
Mammano, Julie.
Rhinos who snowboard / by Julie Mammano
p.   cm.
Summary: Snowboarding rhinos check out the weather, head for the
slopes, and spend all day out on the snow-covered mountains.
Includes a glossary of snowboarding lingo.
[1. Snowboarding—Fiction. 2. Rhinoceroses—Fiction.] 1. Title
PZ7.M3117Rf   1997
[E]—dc21   97-1349 CIP
AC

Distributed in Canada by Raincoast Books
9050 Shaughnessy Street, Vancouver, British Columbia V6P 6E5

10 9 8 7 6 5 4 3 2 1

Chronicle Books LLC
85 Second Street, San Francisco, California 94105

www.chroniclekids.com

JULIE MAMMANO

Rhinos Who Snowboard

chronicle books · san francisco

Rhinos who snowboard live for the snow.

SNOW! SNOW! SNOW!

SEASON PASS

They strap on their boards and take a lift to the GNARLIEST peaks.

They BUST OUT fast down the FALL LINE!

They go **TOTALLY AGGRO.**

They **CHARGE** the steepest slopes.

They ride through the backcountry.

They carve perfect POWDER FANS.

Rhinos who snowboard FLOAT STIFFY TAILGRABS.

They catch PHAT AIR over INSANE GAPS.

They plant **HOHOS** off the lip of a windblown **HALFPIPE.**

Rhinos who snowboard are SPIN MASTERS.

They **LAUNCH MAJOR** backflips.

It is so UNCOOL when MOGUL hopping KOOKS botch up their big jumps.

At the end of the day, they take their final run.

Rhinos who snowboard CHILL OUT while loads of PHAT POW DUMP outside.

Tomorrow will be EPIC!

Board Speak

air jump trick

bonk to hit an object on purpose for style

bummer really bad

bust out to start quickly then go fast

charge go for it

chill out relax

dump to snowfall in big amounts

epic really great

faceplant to land on your face

fakie to ride backwards

fall line straight down a slope of a mountain

float to make a big jump

freefall to fall airborne straight down

gnarliest biggest, scariest

halfpipe curve in snow shaped like a tube

hohos two handed handstands

huck to jump wildly

insane gaps big spaces between cliffs or slopes

kooks jerks who ski or snowboard

pow powdery snow

powder fans snow sprayed in the shape of a fan

rude really bad

slams crashes

spin master one who does spin tricks

stiffy with both legs straight

stoked to the max really happy

tailgrabs grab the back of the board

totally aggro fearless

uncool bad

launch to take off on a jump

major very

mogul bump in the snow

phat really big, high, or great

poser pretend snowboarder

Julie Mammano was born and raised in Southern California. She graduated from Biola University in 1984 with a Bachelor of Arts degree. Soon after, she started working as a staff artist for a greeting card company and later as a designer for a children's magazine. Julie is now a freelance artist and illustrator who works in Southern California. Already a surfer, she also enjoys snowboarding.

ALSO BY JULIE MAMMANO

Rhinos Who Surf
Rhinos Who Skateboard
Rhinos Who Play Soccer
Rhinos Who Play Baseball